Puppy Crate Training For Beginners:

The Fast and Fun Way to Crate Train Your Puppy

John Honda

Copyright © 2020 John Honda

All rights reserved. No part of this publication may be reproduced, stored in or introduced into a retrieval system, or transmitted, in any form, or by any means (electronic, mechanical, photocopying, recording, or otherwise) without the prior written permission of the copyright owner of this book and is illegal and punishable by law.

Although the author and publisher have made every effort to ensure that the information in this book was correct at press time, the author and publisher do not assume and hereby disclaim any liability to any party for any loss, damage, or disruption caused by errors or omissions, whether such errors or omissions result from negligence, accident, or any other cause.

Download Your Free Gift Now

Discover the "Brain Game" that Develops Your Dog's Intelligence and Eliminates Bad Behavior…

While Still Having Fun

As a way of saying "Thank You" for your purchase, I'm going to share with you a

Free Gift that is exclusive to readers of Puppy Crate Training for Beginners.

It will help you double your Love and Care for your Puppy!

[Click Here to Check it Out](https://braingamefordogs.groovepages.com/gift/airplane)

https://braingamefordogs.groovepages.com/gift/airplane

Table of Contents

Introduction to Crate Training 1

Chapter 1. Pros and Cons to Crate Training 3

    Benefits of Crate Training Puppies 3

    Does Crate Training Help with House Breaking? 5

    What Age Should You Start Crate Training a Puppy? 6

Chapter 2. Why Should You Crate Train Your Puppy? 8

    Picking the Best Crate for Your Dog 10

    These are the five basic types of dog crates: 12

Chapter 3. Best Place For A Dog Crate 16

Chapter 4. Crate Games And Activities 23

Chapter 5. So Which Crate is Right for you and your Puppy? 26

Chapter 6. Crate Hunting 29

    The Actual Steps 30

Chapter 7. What to do When Your Puppy is whining in the Crate 33

    How to Handle Separation Anxiety When Crate Training Your Puppy 36

    Conclusion 39

Congrats! Note from the Author 40

Introduction to Crate Training

Crate training is generally recognized as one of the best ways to housetrain your puppy. Despite this, there is still a lot of reluctance among pet owners to adopt crate training as part of their training regimen, since they feel that it is in some way cruel to their pet. However, it is important to keep in mind that teaching your dog to accept temporary confinement without anxiety is an important skill for a well-behaved pet, as well as living as part of human society. If crate training is adopted humanely and responsibly, it can have many benefits for both the dog and its owner. These include:

- Providing a 'home away from home' for the pet. The crate will serve not only as a place to rest, away from a stressful environment, but also as the dog's 'den' where he can play with toys.

- Establishing a regular routine that makes training easier. Since dogs will not poop where they sleep, you can take him out after he eats and he will be ready to poop where you designate.

- Making it easier and safer when your dog travels with you. Contrary to the impression that many movies give, the safest place for your dog is not the passenger seat of your car, but in a crate where he is in a stable environment rather than constantly bouncing around inside the vehicle. In addition, having a crate-trained dog will make it easier for you to find accommodations since many hotels and motels will be willing to allow a dog if he can be crated when you are not in the room.

- Ensuring the safety of a new dog. By restricting the puppy from potentially unsafe parts of the house during times when you cannot supervise it, you have an assurance that it will not chew on electric cables or get into other mischief that can be dangerous.

- Restricting the dog's movements when it is not yet properly trained. For example, if you have guests over and your dog has not yet been socialized completely, you can keep your dog in the crate temporarily, or use it to introduce it to new people or pets without the risk that it will engage in aggressive or otherwise undesirable behavior such as biting and jumping.

This book will teach you everything you need to know about using crates to safely and humanely train your new puppy so that it can grow up to be a well-behaved, valued member of your family. The topics discussed in this book include:

- Choosing a crate for your puppy – what you need to keep in mind

- The right way to introduce your dog to its new crate

- What you must never do when crate training your dog

Thank you for downloading this ebook and I hope that it is useful to you!

Chapter 1. Pros and Cons to Crate Training

Benefits of Crate Training Puppies

Crate training your puppy brings multiple benefits for you and your pet. If handled correctly, your puppy will eventually grow to accept the dog crate as his den or "house" and it can be regarded as a place of refuge for your dog to get away from everyone when he needs to. Your puppy should feel secure and safe in its kennel and as long as you don't use it for discipline or leave your pup inside it 24 hours a crate training puppies.

A Crate Can Be Your Puppy's Bed

One way to get your new puppy used to being inside a crate is to use it as a bed at night. You can put a comfy blanket or towel, maybe with a stuffed animal or a clock wrapped up in a towel to simulate a heartbeat. When it is time for bed, lead your puppy to the crate, put it in with a treat or two, and close the door. He/she may protest, but once they get used to sleeping in it, they will consider it their den and learn to enjoy it. They probably will even head to it to take a nap if you leave it open for them to do so. This is to be encouraged because if your puppy loves its crate, it will be easier to use it if you leave the house for a short while or need to use it to take them somewhere.

Housebreaking is Faster, Easier

Dogs normally will not go to the bathroom where they sleep, so if the kennel is your puppy's bed, or where she goes to rest, then s won't go unless of course, you have left her in there so long she can't hold it any longer. If you put your puppy inside the crate for a few minutes or longer, every time you take her out of there you should take the puppy outside to potty, especially if she has been asleep for a while.

Puppies usually have to go after eating and sleeping. So, you should take it outside and encourage it to do so each time you have had it in the crate.

Keeps Your Puppy Out of Both Trouble, Danger

Another benefit for you and your puppy is that a crate will keep it out of trouble, as well as keep it from getting hurt. If you have to leave the house for an hour or so and leave your puppy in its kennel, then it can't get out and chew up your shoes or bite through an electric cord, or any other mischief that puppies are prone to get into. Puppies are curious little beings and will chew or get into anything they can stick their nose or paws into. If you don't want to come home to trash strewn all over the kitchen or shredded foam from your pillows all over the living room or worse yet an electrocuted puppy, then for both your sakes, put your dog in its kennel while you are gone. Once you are home, be sure to take it out to potty!

Transporting your Puppy

If you get your puppy used to the crate, it will also be much easier and less stressful for your puppy if you have to use it to take the puppy someplace. Whether it is a trip to the vet or a trip out of town or even an airplane ride, there is going to be far less stress if your pup is already used to the crate and feels safe and secure while in it. The crate should be like a sanctuary for your pup, and not feel like a trap or a cage.

Does Crate Training Help with House Breaking?

Potty training your new puppy is probably one of the least fun things about having a dog. It can also be sometimes among the hardest, most frustrating things in the world, or if you do it through crate training, it can be much simpler and far less stressful for you personally as well as your dog.

As mentioned earlier, dogs normally won't go to the toilet where they sleep. This is an instinct all dogs have because in the wild it would have lead predators right to their den and put them in danger. So, if you have already established the crate as your puppy's bed, then you are already halfway to successful potty training.

When your puppy first wakes up in the morning, take him/her out immediately and encourage him to go to the toilet. Be sure to wait long enough to see if it has to urinate or poo. You should use a special word that will let the puppy know what you expect. For instance, with my dogs, I would say, "Go bathroom." Then when it does, praise your puppy and bring it back into the house.

Also, if you are getting ready to go anywhere and your pup will be staying in the dog crate, be sure to take it outside again and encourage it to visit the potty before you put it inside the crate, and once again when you take your dog back out. If you get into this habit, the dog will associate these times as times when it needs to go and this will make it much better to get the dog on somewhat of a bathroom schedule.

Whenever your pup is not in the kennel, you still have to watch for signs your pet may have to go, but if it has an accident, don't yell or scold your dog. Just clean it up and be more watchful next time, as dogs won't understand being punished for it since it is already done.

Handling potty training using a crate means fewer messes and more structure for your pup. It won't take long for your puppy to know that going in or out from the crate means that he is going to get a chance to visit the potty. Plus, even if your pup has an accident outside the crate, you are more likely to find it than if you left him alone, so it will also be easier to clean.

The bottom line is that potty training through crate training is the way to go. It is much simpler, faster, and less stressful for everyone.

What Age Should You Start Crate Training a Puppy?

So, you have your new puppy and you wonder if it is old enough to be crate trained since you have heard how great it is and how much it helps with potty training or other benefits. But wait a minute. Your puppy is only 8 weeks old, should he/she be crated?

The answer depends on the reason for crating your pup. If you are doing it to get the puppy used to the kennel, such as using it for his bed at night, then it is old enough and you should let your puppy out to go potty as soon as it wakes up. At less than 12 weeks of age, it probably doesn't have much bladder or sphincter control so you can't leave the pup for hours and hours inside the crate. The pup will just go on itself and be miserable.

But, you can leave puppy in the crate for short periods of time and at night for sleeping as long as you take it out to go to the bathroom as soon as possible in the morning. Puppies that are less than 12 weeks old have to go to the bathroom 12-18 times a day so you really have to be on guard to the signs and you can't just lock puppy up in a crate all day and expect his little bladder to hold out. You are just asking for trouble.

So, the answer is to only use it for more than a few minutes if it is under 12 weeks old, except at night when you are using the crate for his bed.

Puppies under 4 months of age do not have much bladder or sphincter control. Puppies under 3 months have even less. Very young puppies under 9 weeks should not be crated, as they need to excrete very frequently (usually 8-12 times or more daily).

Chapter 2. Why Should You Crate Train Your Puppy?

Crate training has been termed as one of the most important things to do for your dog. Some dog owners seem uncomfortable with the whole idea, at least initially. Here are some of the reasons why crate training your dog is considered important.

It is a Safe Haven

Dogs have it in their nature to stay in dens. When you consider the atmosphere of many homes, you can understand that from time to time your dog will need to pull away from all the activities and spend some alone time in a "den."

Having a dog crate serves this purpose. When your dog climbs into the crate, you should let them have some quality time on their own. This will lead to an emotionally gratified dog that will connect with you at an even deeper level. Also, the crate serves as a refuge to the dog whenever they face a threat.

Housetraining Purposes

Dog owners get frustrated when their dog relieves themselves without paying attention to where they are. Crates are vital equipment, as they help you teach your dog how to control their bladder and bowel movement.

When you housetrain your dog, you must exercise patience and resist from punishing your dog when they fail to adhere to your rules. The whole exercise must hinge on patience and persistence. In the end, your dog will become disciplined enough to relieve himself where you want them to. After all, dogs hate dwelling in a soiled environment.

Safety

It can be nerve-wracking to go to work and leave your dog behind, imagining all the crazy things your dog might be up to. A dog crate provides a sanctuary for your dog.

This way, you can enclose the dog in the haven when you are not around. Also, when you are having a renovation in your house or cleaning it, you may keep the dog in the crate as it would be dangerous for them to frolic around, considering that sharp tools might harm them.

Fun

When you get your dog a crate, one of the things you must provide is a toy. This will ensure that the dog will have something to play with as the hours roll by.

When your dog has some toys in their crate, they can easily chew on those toys instead of other valuable things in your household like furniture. Also, crates are great for feeding your dog. Ideally, you should put the food toward the end. When you combine food and attractive toys, your dog will be very entertained.

Traveling

It can be quite hectic to move around when the dog is not restrained. For instance, it is convenient to have your dog in the crate when you are traveling by road, as opposed to them prancing around in the car, which would pose safety concerns.

A dog crate ensures that your dog is confined in a comfortable environment, in which they can function without facing constraints. The preparation encourages the dog to develop a positive feeling toward the crate so that eventually, they become attached to the crate and want to spend most of their time there.

Guests

Not to mean that guests are allergic to dogs, but for some reason, you might prefer to have the dog held away when your guests are around. If you lack a dog crate, you will not be able to do it without hurting your dog's feelings. A crate serves as a good place to put your dog when you have guests over.

Easier Vet Visits

Sometimes, the dog might come down with an illness that requires them to stay with the vet for more than a day. In such instances, it does the vet a world of good that the dog is crate trained. The dog will also be far more at peace in new territory when they are confined in their crate.

For Calming Your Dog

Some dogs can really escalate their feelings and actions. In such cases, a significant amount of damage is done. A crate is crucial for managing such dogs. You may put your dog in the crate as a way of calming them down. A crate-trained dog responds well to time-outs.

Evacuation

As long as you live in a modern house, there are various potential disasters and emergencies. It is easier to evacuate a dog who has been crate trained than the one who is not. If your dog is handed over to new owners, the separation hurts them less because they are still in their own crate and surrounded by familiar items.

Picking the Best Crate for Your Dog

A dog crate gives your dog his own personal space. There are several things to consider before selecting a dog crate: how you plan to use it, the age of your dog, their personality, and their breed.

The practical concerns include: how easy it is to clean and carry around, and whether the color and material of the crate align with your aesthetic taste.

Dog crates come in a wide range of sizes, styles, designs, and materials. All dog crates will hold your dog and help with potty training.

Picking the dog crate that is best for you will depend on the size of your dog and other variables. Here are some of the questions that you should ask yourself before you purchase a crate:

- Will the crate get moved around or will it stay in one place?
- Will you travel long distances with the crate?
- Does your dog have the habit of chewing on things?
- Will it be easy to clean up this crate?
- How does the crate fit into your home and decor?

The biggest mistake that most dog owners make is buying a crate that is a few sizes too big. Before you buy a crate, you should first measure the size of your dog.

To get their height, you should measure from the top of their shoulders to their paws; to get their length, you should measure from the tip of their nose to the tip of their tail. The ideal crate should allow your dog to stand up, sit down, and turn around comfortably. The door should be wide enough for the dog to go in and out without any difficulties. (Refer to Chart Below)

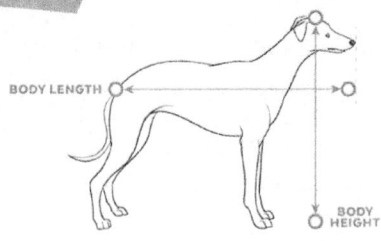

CRATE SIZE CHART
frisco. better pet goods
FRISCO STANDARD CRATES · SINGLE DOOR

SIZE	CRATE DIMENSIONS (in)	MAXIMUM HEIGHT (in)	MAXIMUM LENGTH (in)	BREED RECOMMENDATIONS
18"	18 L x 12 W x 14 H	10	14	Chihuahua, Pomeranian
22"	22 L x 13 W x 15.5 H	11.5	18	Toy Poodle, Yorkshire Terrier
24"	24 L x 18 W x 19.25 H	15.25	20	Havanese, Pug
30"	30 L x 19 W x 21 H	17	26	French Bulldog, Miniature Pinscher
36"	36 L x 23 W x 25 H	21	32	Beagle, Bulldog
42"	42 L x 28 W x 30 H	26	38	Golden Retriever, Pitbull
48"	48 L x 30 W x 32.5 H	28.5	46	German Shepherd, Doberman

*Please Note: For a correct fit, it is necessary to measure your dog's body height and length, and compare to the chart above. Body height can be measured while your dog is standing or seated. If your pet's measurements exceed the maximum height or body length, we recommend ordering the next size up.

These are the five basic types of dog crates:

1. Plastic crates

2. Wire crates

3. Heavy-duty crates

4. Soft-sided crates

5. Cute crates

Plastic Crates

It takes two pieces of molded plastic to make this type of crate. The top and bottom are held in place by plastic fasteners, and there is a metal-wire door.

Some crates designed for puppies tend to have a plastic door which is a huge drawback, considering that puppies like chewing on things. Most plastic crates have a moat that runs around the edge of the floor which traps the dog's urine and drains it.

Advantages of plastic crates

- The space is comfortable
- Makes it easier to travel with your dog
- Good at containing puppies
- Available in different colors
- The top half can come off easily and get stacked with the bottom half for easier storage

Disadvantages of plastic crates

- On warm days, it can get hot in there
- It limits your dog's scope of vision which might disorient them
- Not very aesthetically pleasing

Wire Dog Crates

For the most part, these crates are made of panels of wire, but the floor is made of plastic. The material that is used is sturdy, and it also discourages the habit of chewing up things.

Advantages of wire crates

- It has great ventilation which allows dogs to be at ease. The wire crate is perhaps the best choice for dogs living in hot climates.

- You can section off the crate using a divider. This allows you to increase the area occupied by the dog as they grow older.

- It can be folded. This proves important when carrying or storing the crate.

- The removable floor makes it easy to clean.

Disadvantages of wire crates

- They produce more noise than plastic crates when your dog moves around

- Some models are weak enough for a dog to break free.

- The design is not attractive

Soft-sided crates

Soft-sided crates are considered the most portable crates. It is available in a wide range of styles, sizes, and materials.

Advantages of soft-sided crates

- It is lightweight, which makes it easy to carry your dog around.

- Ideal for containing a dog with serious separation anxiety.

- The best for traveling and camping. Due to its lightweight status, you can bring your dog along for road travels and even camping.

- It is very easy to store since it can be folded.

Disadvantages of soft-sided crates

- Hard to clean up in case of a major potty accident.

- Some dogs can chew their way out.

- Some dogs might figure out how to open the zip door.

Heavy-duty crates

These crates are designed using heavy-duty material. They are available in various styles and colors.

Advantages of heavy-duty crates

- There is almost a zero chance that the dog will break free.
- They are the most suitable for traveling by air.

Disadvantages of heavy-duty crates

- It is expensive, but keep in mind that they are made of sturdy material which justifies the expense.

Cute Crates

As the name suggests, the cute crates are aesthetically pleasing, compared to the rest. They are mostly made of wood and exotic materials.

Advantages of cute crates

- It has a tasteful design.
- It is designed for comfort.

Disadvantages of cute crates

- Destructive dogs can chew at the wood

Chapter 3. Best Place For A Dog Crate

Training a puppy or an adult dog in a crate is a great way to protect them from harm and can provide you with complete peace of mind when your puppy is home alone.

However, before you start crate training on your puppy, you will need to know where to place the crate and what to put in it. Your puppy's crate should be in a good location, a comfortable and welcoming place where it can always happily retreat to.

In this section, we will explain what the best locations for crates are and what should or should not be placed in there.

The Best Location To Place A Dog Crate In Your Home

We know that dogs are very sociable animals: they must be close to their owners and feel integrated into the daily life of the family. Remember that being in a crate should give the dog a positive experience, it should never be considered a punishment.

For puppies, it is a good idea to place the crate in your bedroom at night to ensure it feels safe, secure, and not abandoned. They will get great comfort and a feeling of safety and security being able to sleep near the family especially in the early days of being in a new home.

After all, placing the crate in a busy area that will make the puppy feel like a family member is the best choice.

The exact location differs from one house to another: it can be the living room, the kitchen, or any other place with good traffic. If your puppy likes to go there or you train him to get used to the crate, putting him where the action is will make the dog feel like he is included in the family.

What about my bedroom?

If you have a puppy, it's a good idea to move the crate to your bedroom at night. Leaving it in another room while you sleep can give the puppy a feeling of helplessness, stress, and insecurity, which can lead to whining and crying. If you don't want to move the crate from the living room to the bedroom every day, buy a second crate, and eliminate the hassle.

A quiet corner

Regrettably, not all puppies are as energetic and outgoing as we would like - some remain anxious and stressed even when they become adults. Some dogs do not like guests, loud music, family celebrations, and dinners and prefer to have a safe and quiet place, away from all the hassle. For these dogs or puppies, placing the crate in a quiet corner of the house is the best idea: they will have their "time alone" in which they can retreat whenever necessary.

Tips To Consider When Choosing The Location

- Make sure your pet's crate is away from the fireplace or radiator. The motive is rather simple: you don't want your pet's blankets to be caught in the fire and leave you without your beloved pet. This is significant if you are using a custom wooden crate.

- The area should not be draughty. As in places with heat sources, areas of excessive drainage can have a very negative effect on the health of your pet over time. The place should be dry and not damp or windy.

- Keep the crate away from direct sunlight. Some homes have large windows that allow lots of sunlight to enter the room, and placing the crate in front of that window can be deadly, especially if you leave the dog locked in and leave the house.

- Avoid extremely hot or cold places. Like humans, dogs love places that are neither too cold nor too hot, but fair.

Moving The Crate Or Purchasing A Second One?

If the idea of having the crate in more than one position seems appropriate to you, the following question arises: should you move the existing crate from one room to another or buy another? Since we do not know your particular situation, we can provide you with a few things to think about that can help you:

- Is the crate portable enough to be easily moved back and forth?
- Are you ready to spend extra money on a second crate?
- How long does the dog sleep in your room? If he is only there for a short time, one crate should suffice.
- If you decide to buy a second crate, consider its other uses (if it can be used in cars and planes, for example).

What To Put In A Puppy Crate

An empty crate is not a welcoming place: some objects must be placed inside for maximum comfort. In this part of the book, we will see what types of bedding and toys, owners should put in their dogs' crates.

Bedding for puppies

Soft-stuffed bedding, towels, and blankets are easily chewed, torn apart, and ingested by puppies. The main danger here is that puppies can choke on these things or even have an internal blockage - this is why puppy owners should be especially careful when purchasing new beddings for their puppies.

Puppies' toys

Allowing your puppy to play with toys while inside of the crate can be very beneficial for their mental and physical health, but like the beddings, these toys must be durable and long-lasting. Leaving your puppy with stuffed toys, soft or strident is not good since the puppy can destroy it easily and swallow small pieces.

Indestructible toys

Fortunately, the current market offers many so-called "indestructible" toys (for breeds like Pitbulls), which are more than suitable for crates puppies. Most of these toys are incredibly durable, but also empty, allowing the owner to fill up with the puppy's favorite snacks. As you can imagine, this keeps your puppy busy because they will chew a lot to get to their treats.

Letting your young dog play with these types of toys in a crate has several advantages:

- Having an alternate object that they can chew on as much as they want prevents them from damaging the beddings.

- A toy is a great item to past time: it keeps your puppy from being bored while it is confined.

- By surrounding the puppy with familiar objects, it will feel less alone and more comfortable.

- Toys can add fun to your puppy's time in the crate. It is an excellent tool to accustom the puppy to its crate.

- This helps the puppy to know which items they can chew and which they cannot, which means that they will be less likely to chew various household items when they get out of the crate.

Should I Leave Food And Water In A Puppy's Crate?

As far as water is concerned, the general rule is that it is not recommended to leave the water inside the puppy's crate, especially if you are potty-training the puppy. The reason is that constant access to water can increase the number of accidents inside the crate: puppies' bladders fill up very quickly.

However, there may be occasions when you will need to do this. For example, leaving your puppy confined during the hot season requires you to leave some water if you don't want your puppy to get heatstroke. For such situations, it is essential to have adequate equipment to provide water to your puppy. The best decision is to purchase a bowl mounted in a box, as they are difficult to tip over and not spill.

Likewise, it is not recommended to leave food in the kennel during your absence. Not only can this create a real mess, but the most important thing is that your puppy has a fixed feeding routine: having established meals is better than eating "freely" when training and raising your new puppy. Letting the puppy eat as much as possible can almost always lead to more frequent accidents – which you do not want.

On the other hand, it is good to feed your puppy its main meals inside the kennel: this increases the positive association it will have with being in the crate as time passes.

Should I Cover A Puppy Crate?

Regrettably, there is no better answer to this question: some puppies or dogs like the indoor crate and others don't, so it depends entirely on your puppy. The wooden or plastic models are already tightly closed, while the metal (metal boxes) models are much more open and cannot give your puppy the touch it instinctively likes.

A covered crate gives the puppy or dog a feeling of security, comfort, and intimacy and can be very useful in reducing the stimulation of anxious and easily distracted puppies by the things going on around them.

Some puppies or dogs, however, like the feeling of space and openness and like to be aware of their surroundings at all times.

These puppies can become very stressed and anxious when their crate is covered with something.

There is only one way to tell if your puppy likes to cover the kennel: try it. As with everything else, the key is going gradually. Start by covering the ceiling for only a few days, then move slowly to most of the box, covering one side after the other. Avoid covering all sides: the puppy will need ventilation to control the fresh air and temperature. Also, always be with them while they get used to it, and don't leave the kennel covered if you leave the house.

There is a good chance that the puppy will resist at first. If the puppy continues to moan and scratch the cap after a few days of gradual introduction, it will be necessary to stop the process and remove the cap completely. Your puppy may be suffering from separation anxiety and having them in a crate causes great stress. On the other hand, if they show no sign of distress and have no trouble sleeping on a covered crate, they like the feeling that the blanket gives them and you can leave them in that position safely.

What Should I Use As A Cover?

Most people use things like old sheets and towels, and these are perfectly fine. However, it is essential to make sure that your puppy cannot pull them into the crate and chew them, as this can cause suffocation.

A good idea would be to place the crate into the corner of the room where the two sides are covered by the walls and placing a wooden board above the crate, as it not only covers the roof, but also makes the crate surface looks great. This has the benefit of your puppy not being able to pull the wooden board into the crate instead of using a blanket.

On the other hand, if you are not interested in using a wooden board, you can also buy an adequate blanket at any pet store. These are made to fit different sizes of crates and are very easy to attach, with some of them having useful panels that allow you to adjust the amount of space covered. They are available in multiple styles, so it's very easy to find one that won't spoil the overall aesthetic of your home.

Regardless of the option you select, be sure to leave at least one side of the crate exposed for ventilation.

Chapter 4. Crate Games And Activities

Whether you are training a child how to count numbers or teaching a dog to sit in a crate for a while, games can make the training more enjoyable and less of a drag. Games make the training more rewarding for the puppy and certainly more interactive for them. If you ask any teacher, you can guarantee that they will tell you kids learn quicker if you keep them motivated with games.

The Basic Crate Game:

In the first section, we introduced the first activity to teach and encourage your dog to spend more time in the crate. The most basic form of this activity is to throw your dog's favorite treat into the cage and shout cage, or the command word you have chosen. You can change this activity to suit your own dog's personality but you should always make sure that the aim is to get the dog spending as much time as possible in the crate. Once the dog starts to get comfortable in the crate you can start to close the door for short periods of time whilst offering lots of praise. Keep this going and make the dog spend longer and longer periods in the crate. This is one of the basic activities but there are many available and you can always create your own if you are experienced with training.

"Let Me In " Game:

Like most puppy training, crate training will involve lots of treats and this game is no different. At first, you should have been putting the tasty dog treats that your pet loves into the crate and let him go inside to get the food. Praise the dog and heap affection on him when he goes inside and stop when he comes out. With this game, the idea is to put the treats in the back of the crate but clearly visible and lock the cage. It may seem mean and look like your teasing him but the puppy will see the treats and beg to go inside. He might even paw at the door to try and get inside and this will plant the idea of positive associations inside his head. He will consider this a good place where he gets his favorite treats and he will want to come here again.

Share a movie:

One thing we want to avoid when crate training is the dog believing that he will be put in the cage only when you are leaving. Next time you sit down to watch a movie or television, place the crate next to you and whenever the puppy is relaxed you can give him a tiny treat or more. This way the puppy will think of the crate as somewhere he can relax and not just somewhere he will be stored. This is a great way to get the puppy comfortable when just chilling out at home and the dog will not automatically think you are leaving him when you order him into the crate.

Clicker training:

Clicker training is a proven method and something you can do in order to help in the future. You should first get a decent clicker from a pet store and if you intend to use this method you would need to be extremely consistent with the clicking.

To start crate training using a clicker, wait until the dog is hungry and beckon him to the crate. You should have already been putting food in the crate so the dog is comfortable with it so he should already associate the crate with food and happiness. Throw some treats inside and lock the door for a very short while. Make sure you are praising the dog and giving it affection. Sometimes your dog might respond better to a toy being thrown inside but only the owner will know that. When he goes inside to get the treat, make sure you click so the dog can hear. As long as the dog is inside the crate, keep clicking and treating the dog. The clicking and treating is the most important part; you should only ever click when giving the treat to make the dog associate clicking with treating; this is the principle of the activity.

After a little training, your dog should be more confident with going into the crate for longer periods of time. You can then start clicking and treating when the dog waits patiently to leave. If they want to leave and make a fuss about it by moaning or barking, no click and no treat. If they wait patiently for you to let them free, click and treat. You should decide before you start if you want to use a clicking technique as you shouldn't just introduce the clicking halfway through.

The Waiting Game:

This one takes a pretty patient dog and an even more patient owner. This trick teaches obedience and encourages the dog to think that being in the crate is awesome because you get treated. Once your dog is in the crate, place a treat outside and wait for his reaction. If he sits calmly and patiently you can start to open the door. If he rises to jump out when he sees enough room then close the door again. Repeat the process until you can fully open the door and the dog will wait without leaping out. You can click when the dog gets the treat if you are using a clicking technique.

Chapter 5. So Which Crate is Right for you and your Puppy?

The next question on your mind should be "Which crate is right for you and your puppy?" There are three major types of crates that are available in the market today.

1. Flight kennel – This is the number one preferred crate for puppy training as it also doubles as a means of transporting your puppy from one place to another. These crates are often made out of plastic and are light enough to carry around and easy enough to clean should there be any mishaps during training. They're also pretty well ventilated and your puppy can be directed to see in one general direction although there are small slats provided at the side.

2. Rigid fabric crates – Other pet owners would argue that these fabric crates aren't entirely that practical as the puppy will eventually outgrow them or tend to gnaw at the material and destroy it. Furthermore, fabric crates can't contain a rambunctious puppy. Just remember though that if you do use rigid fabric crates, these are not meant to serve as cages. Since we are talking about crate training, using a rigid fabric crate for short periods of time will serve you well.

3. Collapsible metal crates – Arguably the best type of crate to train your puppy in, these collapsible metal crates can serve another purpose which is as a temporary or semi-permanent dog cage until your puppy is big enough to have a permanent one. Since puppies grow at a surprising rate, you might want to choose one that's two or three times bigger than your puppy. Just block off the unused sections until your puppy is big enough before you make the necessary adjustments. Collapsible metal crates are also fully ventilated and allow your puppy a 360-degree view of everything around it.

Whichever crate you choose to use with your puppy should be fine. Just remember that these crates are not meant to be permanent housing for your puppies and should only be used for crate training purposes. Furthermore, keep your crates clean regularly so that your puppy will always view it as a nice safe place where they can retire to when they feel sleepy or tired.

As a basic rule of thumb: make sure that the crate has enough space for your puppy to stand, sit and turn around in. The reason for this very limited space is dogs do not like to soil their dens. Most people say to buy a crate that your full-grown dog can sit and turn around in but this can be really big for a puppy. So if you only want to buy one crate then try to block off the extra space in the crate so it doesn't feel too big for your puppy. The other option is to buy two different crates one big enough for the puppy and then a bigger one for your full-grown dog. Just remember that you want to find something that is cozy and comfortable for your puppy and ultimately your dog.

Potential Problems you Might Face with Crate Training

You might face many potential problems during crate training. Once again, extreme patience and vigilance are essential.

Puppies have small bladders and it is quite impossible for them to hold it in especially at a young age. To reduce the risk of your puppy making a mess inside the crate, make sure you take him out every 20 minutes or so. Mark your progress and slowly increase the duration of time that they are inside their crate before taking them out again to relieve themselves.

When they do make a mess, clean the crate immediately. There is no need to admonish the puppy since that will only provide a negative experience. Use a non-ammonia-based cleaning liquid, and continue the crate training program.

Also, some puppies may develop extreme boredom and end up chewing on their crate's insides if left alone. To avoid this from happening, make sure your pet has his favorite toy with him to alleviate his boredom and feeling of isolation.

Things to Remember About Crate Training

1. Crate training should be done as soon as you get your puppy.

2. Crate training is not meant to serve as a punishment.

3. Try your best never to leave your puppy or dog inside the crate for longer than 4 hours (exceptions to this rule are: when it's time for sleep and when you really have to go out either to work or to run some errands).

4. Always make sure that each training session is a positive experience for your puppy. Always reward good behavior with lots of praises and treats.

5. Remember that your crate is not meant to be a dog cage. Crates need to have limited space and it would be inhumane to keep your dogs inside a crate for an extended period of time.

6. Never force your puppy into a crate, allow him to enter and exit the crate on his own.

7. Get the right sized crate or make divisions inside to ensure that the space inside is just right for the puppy to sit, stand and turn around in. Any smaller than that and your puppy will feel trapped. Any bigger than that and your puppy might start treating half of the crate as his toilet.

8. Last but not least: invest in a good pair of gloves, a mop, and some ammonia-based cleaning solutions to clean up after your puppy should there be any mishaps that occur along the way.

Chapter 6. Crate Hunting

Now that you are familiar with the philosophy behind crate training, basic dog psychology, as well as the potential problems and benefits you may encounter during the process, you are ready to equip yourself with the necessary materials for crate training. This chapter will help you select the right kind of crate for your dog and puppy. It will also give you additional information on what other materials you might need to use during the process.

Selecting the right crate for Fido

There are a few things you should consider before you decide on the perfect crate for your canine companion.

First, if you are getting a puppy, then you should keep in mind that that pup will grow rapidly in the following weeks, especially if is of the large or medium breeds. Therefore, you should choose a crate that will cater to the size of your puppy once he or she is fully grown. You can consult dog books regarding this, or ask fellow dog owners about the crate size they use for their big dogs. For toy dogs, you can purchase a small or medium-sized crate, still depending on the maximum height and width of your dog.

Second, consider the materials that were used to construct the crate. Are they non-toxic? Is the crate durable? Are there small attachments on the crate that your dog might chew off?

There are different types of crates available in pet shops everywhere. The most popular one is the plastic, traveler's crate. These crates are usually sold with a guarantee that they are safe for air and sea travel. They are also easy to clean and assemble. They come in different sizes, and the largest ones can comfortably provide shelter for a full-grown German Shepherd Dog.

Another type of crate is the collapsible crate with walls made of tough cloth. They are usually best for puppies or toy dogs. There are also collapsible metal pens that can be attached to each other to expand the space for your dogs. These indoor metal pens are best used for a dam and her puppies during their first two months of life.

Other materials you might need for crate training

If you are training a puppy, then you should secure a piece of cloth or towel that has the scent of the pup's siblings and parents. This will help decrease the loneliness of the puppy on its first night in your house.

You should also be ready with rags for cleaning up after your puppy or dog in case they soil their crate, or the area around it, due to stress or excitement. Treats and dog foods are good lures for any dog, and will help your new canine companion feel more at ease. You should also have some chew toys to help take your dog's stress away as it adjusts to its new environment. In addition, chew toys also help puppies learn which objects can be played with, and which things are to be left alone.

The Actual Steps

Finally, you are ready to begin crate training your puppy or dog. This chapter will take you through the process step by step. Hopefully, by the end of this chapter, you will know exactly how to engage the interest of your canine friend, and successfully teach him or her that the crate is one of the best places to be.

Step 1 – Introduce the crate to your dog or puppy

Let your dog or pup sniff, lick and paw the crate. This is part of their exploration and is necessary for the dog to realize that the crate is neither a threat nor a toy. This will also allow the dog's scent to rub off on the crate, and will therefore make it easier for him to associate his den with the crate.

You can leave your dog and the crate in the same room for increasing periods of time. After some time, your dog should have gained enough interest to explore the inside of the crate. Do not shut the dog in his or her crate the moment you see him/her enter. Remember that you want to make being in the crate a pleasurable experience for your dog. Let him enter and leave the crate for the time being, until such time that the dog is completely at ease with it.

Step 2 – Make the crate a comfortable, happy place to be

If your pup or dog shows little or no interest in the crate, you can help make it a more comfortable, enticing place to be by adding treats or toys. You can also place a soft blanket (or the towel with the siblings and parents' scent for puppies) in the crate to make it warm and inviting. Some dog owners also allow their dogs to take their meals inside their crates.

Step 3 – Introduce the command word

Once your pup or dog is comfortable with the crate, you should introduce the use of a command word or phrase like "Home!" or "Go home!" Other dog owners use the word "Kennel" or "Crate".

Whichever command word you choose, make sure you are consistent with its use. Also, when giving the command word, make sure you are using a happy but firm tone of voice.

Step 4 – Associate the command word with a specific action

Make a sweeping gesture with your hand towards the open crate and give the command word. Once your pup or dog shows signs of advancing towards the crate, even if he or she does it hesitantly, praise and reward your dog. Practice this every day, as often as possible.

Your pup or dog should soon be able to associate the command word with moving towards the crate. You should then encourage your dog to enter the crate by using his or her favorite toy or treat as a reward.

Step 5 – Gradually increase the time that your pup or dog is expected to stay in the crate

For the first few training sessions, let your pup or dog remain in the crate for a few minutes only. Let him or her out afterward, and play with or feed your dog. Repeat the command word and gesture, and reward your dog as you deem fit.

Gradually lengthen the amount of time you leave your pup or dog in his or her crate. If your dog starts to whine or cry, do not let him or her out immediately. Wait for your dog to calm down, then slowly approach the crate, and let your dog out without creating much fuss. This should teach your dog that being left in the crate or being allowed to leave the crate is not a big deal, and thus should not be whined or cried about.

Reward your puppy or dog every time he or she stays quietly in the crate. Remember that no dog should be left in their crate for the whole day. Let your puppy or dog out when they start to make noises because they need to eliminate. As you spend time with your canine friend, you will soon be able to tell when he or she is whining for attention or out of need.

As the saying goes, practice makes perfect. Be patient when crate training your puppy or dog. Keep focused on your goal, and you will soon have a dog who willingly enters and leaves the crate when given the command word.

Chapter 7. What to do When Your Puppy is whining in the Crate

A puppy communicates his needs through cries, just like an infant. When you put your puppy in a crate, he will express his discomfort by crying, and it could take days for him to adjust to the new environment.

Whenever your puppy whines, be careful how you handle him because your response could affect his future behaviors. Here are some of the reasons that drive your puppy into whining and how to make him stop.

- Sickness

When your puppy whines all the time, it could be an indication that he is physically or emotionally unwell. Some of the symptoms to look out for include loss of appetite, diarrhea, lethargy, dizziness, vomiting, and shortness of breath.

If the puppy has bitten, licked, or scratched himself excessively around a certain area of his body, it is indicative of an infection, allergy, parasitic attack, and other skin issues.

If your puppy becomes withdrawn and recoils when you touch him, it is a sign that he is in a world of physical and emotional pain. When you discover any of these symptoms, you should take him to a vet for medical attention.

- Loneliness

The puppy may be struggling with the separation from his parents. This results in whining as a way of sending out an alarm in case the mother can hear him and come to his rescue.

When you are dealing with an emotionally hurting puppy, the whining is usually low-pitched and never-ending. The best way to make him stop is to comfort him by making him see you a lot more. You can carry off the crate to a part of your house where you may interact with him while you are engaged in other things.

- Fear

Various things about the new environment could trigger fear in your puppy. This will make your puppy whine. Inspect the crate and ensure there is nothing wrong. Also, reassure the puppy that everything is alright by stroking him and giving him treats.

- Hunger

Your puppy could also whine due to hunger. Once you give him something to feed on, and he runs to the food like a rat to cheese, then you can be sure that it is hunger. If he ignores the food, it could mean something else is the cause of his discomfort.

- Boredom

Another reason why the puppy could whine is due to boredom. Puppies love having a partner to play with to expend their energy. In the absence of a partner, toys will do. Get them a toy that piques their interest, and they will turn to it to fight the boredom away.

Here are more tips to make your puppy stop crying when you are not sure what the crying is all about:

- Take him to the potty

Perhaps your puppy wants to relieve himself and is trying to get your attention. If he whines in the crate, carry him off to the potty. As soon as he relieves himself, carry him back into his crate without any distractions.

- Play with him

Try to play with him and see how he reacts. This is likely going to get him into a good mood. Playing for a long duration will tire him out and make him want to sleep, which will put an end to his whining.

- Put a sheet over the wire crate

In as much as wire crates are great for ventilation purposes, they are uncomfortable to a certain extent, especially during the night. Spreading a sheet over the wire crate will make your puppy feel more at ease, but you have to be careful in how you tuck away the ends because some puppies will not mind chewing at the sheet.

- Bring the crate to your room

If all your attempts to make him stop crying bear no fruits, you might as well consider bringing the crate into your room. This is certainly going to make him stop whining, especially when he is enveloped by your scent.

- Discourage whining

A puppy is at an impressionable stage. You can use psychological tricks to modify his behavior.

First of all, when he whines, make him stop and then praise him for not whining. You may give him treats and stroke him gently for not whining.

Stop praising him and turn away when he whines. This will condition him to believe that he will only receive praise when he is not whining. Since he is at an impressionable stage, he will want to please you by doing what appears to make you happy.

Here are the two things not to do when your dog whines:

- Do not shout at him. In the worst-case scenario, your puppy could misinterpret this as hostility and become scared. On the other hand, he could also perceive this as interest on your part and carry on with the whining, under the illusion that you are enjoying this activity too.

- Do not use a shock collar. A shock collar is a terrible way of making your dog stop whining. It could hurt him and make him resent being held in the crate.

How to Handle Separation Anxiety When Crate Training Your Puppy

Dogs crave for their owner's attention. They hate it when their owner leaves them alone. For instance, when you leave for work your dog will probably make you feel guilty to look at you with pitiful eyes. Some other dogs will react more aggressively.

Dogs suffering from extreme separation anxiety will bark endlessly, try to ruin everything in their path, and relieve themselves around the house. In some cases, they may even injure themselves as they try to escape.

First of all, you have to establish whether your dog is suffering from separation anxiety or if he is just bored. When your dog is not getting stimulated enough, he can easily get bored and will resort to entertaining himself through barking and chewing at things.

You also have to find out whether your dog is exhibiting true separation anxiety or just 'learned' separation anxiety. Learned separation anxiety is caused by low self-control, and the behaviors that he exhibits are merely simulated. However, when a dog experiences true separation anxiety, he gets stressed whenever his owner is absent.

Signs of separation anxiety:

- Dedicating himself to destroying things
- Trying to get away from home while you are absent

- Relieving himself around the house even though he is potty trained
- Wearing pitiful eyes when you are about to leave the house
- Howling and barking during the day
- Purposely inflicting self-harm
- Acting clingy
- Barking and jumping when you finally come back home

Stop making a big deal out of leaving or arriving at home

Dog owners unknowingly trigger separation anxiety when they make a big deal of leaving or arriving home. Now, this makes your dog more conscious of your absence.

Ceremonial departures and arrivals can affect your dog's capacity to withstand your absence. When you have to leave for work in the morning, resist making a loud gesture that announces your intent to leave like grabbing car keys theatrically. When you come back, do not rush to pet him.

The Power of Exercise

Your dog has a lot of energy, and when he lacks a creative way of spending it, he might resort to raising hell and chewing at things. One of the best ways of spending your dog's energy is to take him out for a walk before you leave.

This exercise will relieve his anxiety and improve his mood and finally when you leave he will be too tired to complain. Introduce new challenges during the walk and make it as eventful as possible.

Leave behind a personal item with your puppy

Dogs have a strong sense of smell. They recognize your smell. When you leave behind a personal item of yours, the scent will remind your puppy of you. It will help comfort him whenever he feels unsafe. You may opt to leave behind a blanket or pillow.

The Charm of Toys

Nothing excites a puppy more than playtime. You could get him a puzzle toy to play with throughout the day.

Before you leave, give him a toy that challenges his skills. He will focus on the toy and have less time to mourn your departure.

Toys provide an escape from boredom as they cater to your puppy's need for stimulation. You might want to buy various puzzle toys to keep your puppy from getting bored.

Give him a different set of toys every day. Your departure will still be a bitter pill to swallow, but it will signify the start of games.

Be Consistent

It can be difficult to establish a routine, especially where puppies are concerned, but it is a sure way of handling separation anxiety. When a dog settles into a routine, he is far less affected by your absence. Make him anticipate walking, feeding, playing, and sleeping.

Take Him to a Daycare

Daycares are great for the social development of your dog. Find out a convenient daycare around your area of residence, and take him there. Track his development. Keep in mind that some dogs are terrified of populated areas.

Contact a Dog Behaviorist

If your dog is battling extreme separation anxiety, consider taking him to a dog behaviorist and trainer. Tell him about your dog's tendencies and explore the various solutions available.

Conclusion

Remember that anything worth doing is worth doing well, and crate training is no exception. With the information in this book and a lot of patience, you should be able to successfully pick out the right crate, understand all the benefits of crate training, and develop valuable methods of training your dog.

Regardless of age, size, or breed, any dog is capable of being crate trained, and as you have probably already learned, it is a mutually beneficial experience for both you and your beloved pet.

If you have chosen the proper crate, and spent the necessary time training your dog with it, you may feel that he or she has earned the right to no longer be locked in. This is a great accomplishment! However, you should always hold onto your crate just in case there is any slip in behavior, you need to travel with your dog, or just so that he or she can still have access to their private space.

Just keep in mind that there is nothing wrong with keeping your dog in their crate for less than four or five hours. It's an important trade-off that keeps them, and your house, safe from any danger or trouble.

So, congratulations on a successful run of crate training, and good luck in the future with you and your pet!

Congrats! Note from the Author

You've reached the end of the book!

Thank you for finishing Puppy Crate Training For Beginners!

Looks like you enjoyed it!

If so, would you mind taking 30 seconds to leave a quick review on Amazon?

We worked hard to bring you books that you enjoy!

Plus, it helps authors like us produce more books like this in the future!

Here's where to go to leave a review now:

{YOUR BOOK PAGE DIRECT LINK}

Customer reviews

4.8 out of 5

399 global ratings

5 star	88%
4 star	9%
3 star	2%
2 star	1%
1 star	1%

How are ratings calculated?

Review this product

Share your thoughts with other customers

Write a customer review

Printed in Great Britain
by Amazon